52 OFFERING PRAYERS & SCRIPTURES

Encouraging the Heart of Giving in the Church

LIFE IMPACT SERIES

FRANK DAMAZIO

CITYBIBLE PUBLISHING

WWW.CITYBIBLEPUBLISHING.COM

"After pastoring for nearly 30 years at one church, I had taught on tithing regularly with marginal success. Since reading the biblical declarations to our congregation, our tithing has increased 15% and has maintained that level for several months. I am delighted for the release that it has given to our people to be faithful to God in giving and experiencing increase financially and spiritually."

— RICHARD PROBASCO
  SENIOR PASTOR, NEW SONG COMMUNITY CHURCH
  PORTLAND, OREGON

PUBLISHED BY CITY BIBLE PUBLISHING

9200 NE Fremont, Portland, Oregon 97220

City Bible Publishing is a ministry of City Bible Church and is dedicated to serving the local church and its leaders through the production and distribution of quality materials. It is our prayer that these materials, proven in the context of the local church, will equip leaders in exalting the Lord and extending His kingdom.

For a free catalog of additional resources from City Bible Publishing, please call 1-800-777-6057 or visit our web site at www.citybiblepublishing.com.

52 Offering Prayers & Scriptures

Cover design by DesignPoint, Inc.
Interior design and typeset by Sharla Cassidy.

First Edition, January 2005

Printed in the United States of America

Table of Contents

During my 29 years of ministry, I spent five years teaching at Portland Bible College and 24 years pastoring. I have taken many offerings and the format was usually the same. I would make a few brief comments: "It's more blessed to give than to receive." "Let's give back to God what He has blessed us with." They were good comments, but they weren't strategic, thus our offering had about the same impact as the other announcements that were made.

This mundane offering routine caused me to begin to question myself. Why do I take offerings this way? Is there a better way to do it? How can I make this a more meaningful stewardship experience? I'm very thankful today that I questioned that routine and began to use these prayer and scripture declarations for our offering time.

This book is a result of that question. Now our offerings are not an intermission time when parents take their children to the nursery and teenagers hurry to the bathroom, but are a time when we join in unity, every person taking part. Now our offerings are full of faith, enthusiasm and joy. The atmosphere of giving is elevated

*as we read out loud and in unity, hearing and speaking
faith. This has changed the way we take the offering;
it has changed the way people give their offering; and
changed the number of people who give an offering.*

*The impact has been two-fold. As a congregation our
tithes and offerings giving has increased. As individuals,
the church has increased in their understanding of the
importance of and the benefits of tithing. Giving has
changed from being an obligatory part of the service
to a joyful time of expectation as we give of ourselves
to God, trusting Him to provide jobs and to bless
businesses and finances.*

*I pray you will greatly benefit from these prayer and
scripture declarations and that God will multiply your
resources many times above what you have ever
received. I pray this strategy will transform your
church and impact the way people think and the
way people give.*

—FRANK DAMAZIO
SENIOR PASTOR, CITY BIBLE CHURCH

Offering Prayers and Scriptures

week
one

As I give in today's offering, I stand on God's promises that the Lord will cause His blessings to come upon me as the windows of heaven are open. Open over my life today all the windows of blessings and supernatural resources. Let it be more than I can handle.

MALACHI 3:10

"Bring all the tithes into the storehouse, that there may be food in My house, and try Me now in this," says the Lord of hosts, "If I will not open for you the windows of heaven and pour out for you such blessing that there will not be room enough to receive it."

DEUTERONOMY 28:8

"The Lord will command the blessing on you in your storehouses and in all to which you set your hand, and He will bless you in the land which the Lord your God is giving you."

week
two

As I give in today's offering, I believe that
the Lord will cause the enemies who rise
up against me to be defeated as He rebukes
the devourer on my behalf. Lord, today
defeat the enemies of doubt, unbelief and
rebuke all my devourers.

MALACHI 3:11

"And I will rebuke the devourer for your sakes, so that he will not destroy the fruit of your ground, nor shall the vine fail to bear fruit for you in the field," says the Lord of hosts.

PSALM 56:12-13

Vows made to You are binding upon me, O God; I will render praises to You, for You have delivered my soul from death. Have You not kept my feet from falling, that I may walk before God in the light of the living?

week
three

As I give in today's offering, I receive all that the Lord will open up to me of His good treasure and give me a surplus of prosperity so I can be generous on all occasions. I choose to honor the Lord today with my firstfruit offering.

PROVERBS 3:9-10

Honor the Lord with your possessions, and with the firstfruits of all your increase; so your barns will be filled with plenty, and your vats will overflow with new wine.

1 CHRONICLES 29:3

"Moreover, because I have set my affection on the house of my God, I have given to the house of my God, over and above all that I have prepared for the holy house, my own special treasure of gold and silver."

week
four

As I give in today's offering, I stand on the word of God and believe the promise that as I sow my seed, God will water and multiply it according to His greatness and goodness. I believe that the principle of multiplication can be released over my life, beginning today.

2 CORINTHIANS 9:6

But this I say: He who sows sparingly will also reap sparingly, and he who sows bountifully will also reap bountifully.

2 CORINTHIANS 9:10

Now may He who supplies seed to the sower... supply and multiply the seed you have.

week
five

As I give in today's offering, I rejoice as I bring to the Lord the firstfruits of my income and my increase. I worship the Lord with a grateful heart, for He has provided faithfully for me and my house. I give willingly and cheerfully.

DEUTERONOMY 26:10

"And now, I have brought the firstfruits of the land which you, O Lord, have given me." "Then you shall set it before the Lord your God, and worship before the Lord your God."

LEVITICUS 22:29

"And when you offer a sacrifice of thanksgiving to the Lord, offer it of your own free will."

week
six

As I give in today's offering, I pray that God will guard my path and help me to walk in His ways and obey His principles all the days of my life. Let my life be fruitful and impacting. Let my giving be governed by the word of God and let my life be blessed with good fruit.

PSALMS 1:1-3

Blessed is the man who walks not in the counsel of the ungodly, nor stands in the path of sinners, nor sits in the seat of the scornful; But his delight is in the law of the Lord, and in His law he meditates day and night. He shall be like a tree planted by the rivers of water, that brings forth its fruit in its season, whose leaf also shall not wither; and whatever he does shall prosper.

2 CORINTHIANS 9:10

Now may He who supplies seed to the sower, and bread for food, supply and multiply the seed you have sown and increase the fruits of your righteousness.

week
seven

As I give in today's offering, I believe that you, O Lord, are a loving, kind, gentle, giving, generous, and liberal God. You will not hold back any good thing for my life. You are my provider.

PSALMS 34:8-10

Oh, taste and see that the Lord is good; blessed is the man who trusts in Him! ... Those who seek the Lord shall not lack any good thing.

ROMANS 8:28-29

And we know that all things work together for good to those who love God, to those who are called according to His purpose. For whom He foreknew, He also predestined to be conformed to the image of His Son, that He might be the first-born among many brethren.

week
eight

As I give in today's offering, I affirm that all the tithe belongs to the Lord and is holy. I have willingly set aside this sacred part of my income according to His word and, by faith and obedience, I now bring my tithe into the storehouse—my local church.

LEVITICUS 27:30

"And all the tithe of the land ... is the Lord's. It is holy to the Lord."

MALACHI 3:10

"Bring all the tithes into the storehouse, that there may be food in My house, and try Me now in this," says the Lord of hosts, "If I will not open for you the windows of heaven and pour out for you such blessing that there will not be room enough to receive it."

week
nine

As I give in today's offering, I acknowledge that God has supreme dominion and universal authority and I am dependent on the grace and power of almighty God. I am a visitor, a sojourner on this planet, a steward of what God allows me to manage. God is the rightful owner of all things.

1 CHRONICLES 29:11-15

"Yours, O Lord, is the greatness, the power and the glory, the victory and the majesty; For all that is in heaven and in earth is Yours; Yours is the kingdom, O Lord, and You are exalted as head over all. Both riches and honor come from You, and You reign over all. In Your hand is power and might; In Your hand it is to make great and to give strength to all. Now therefore, our God, we thank You and praise Your glorious name. But who am I, and who are my people, that we should be able to offer so willingly as this? For all things come from You, and of Your own we have given You. For we are aliens and pilgrims before You, as were all our fathers; our days on earth are as a shadow, and without hope."

week
ten

As I give in today's offering, I stand on
the reliability of God's word. God's word
is perfect, trustworthy, and supernatural.
It is God's voice into my life. I believe that
God's promises in the Scriptures are for
me and by faith I claim them. I will manage
all my resources according to Your word,
O Lord.

NUMBERS 23:19

"God is not a man, that He should lie, nor a son of man, that He should repent. Has He said, and will He not do? Or has He spoken, and will He not make it good?"

JOSHUA 1:8

"This Book of the Law shall not depart from your mouth, but you shall meditate in it day and night, that you may observe to do according to all that is written in it. For then you will make your way prosperous, and then you will have good success."

week
eleven

AS I GIVE IN TODAY'S OFFERING, I REJOICE IN
ALL THE NUMEROUS AND MIRACULOUS BLESSINGS
GOD HAS GIVEN TO ME—MORE BLESSINGS THAN
I COULD HAVE EVER DREAMED OF, MORE BLESSINGS
THAN I DESERVE, MORE BLESSINGS THAN I CAN
COUNT, BLESSINGS OVER EVERY AREA OF MY
LIFE. I REJOICE!

PSALM 103:1-5

Bless the Lord, O my soul; and all that is within me, bless His holy name! Bless the Lord, O my soul, and forget not all His benefits: Who forgives all your iniquities, Who heals all your diseases, Who redeems your life from destruction, Who crowns you with lovingkindness and tender mercies, Who satisfies your mouth with good things, so that your youth is renewed like the eagle's.

week
twelve

AS I GIVE IN TODAY'S OFFERING, I BELIEVE THAT
GOD DESIRES TO GIVE ME SEED TO SOW AND
MULTIPLY MY HARVEST. I BELIEVE THAT IN GOD
ALL THINGS ARE POSSIBLE AT ANY TIME IN ANY
ENVIRONMENT. BY FAITH I RECEIVE TODAY ALL
THAT GOD DESIRES TO RELEASE IN AND THROUGH
MY HANDS TO EXTEND HIS KINGDOM.

LUKE 6:38

"Give, and it will be given to you: good measure, pressed down, shaken together, and running over will be put into your bosom. For with the same measure that you use, it will be measured back to you."

2 CORINTHIANS 9:7-8

So let each one give as he purposes in his heart, not grudgingly or of necessity; for God loves a cheerful giver. And God is able to make all grace abound toward you, that you, always having all sufficiency in all things, may have an abundance for every good work.

week
thirteen

As I give in today's offering, I acknowledge that my life consists of more than the things I have or the things I desire. My life finds meaning in Christ and His eternal kingdom. My life is to be lived as a person who knows where to put my treasures. My giving of my money is an investment into ministry that touches people for eternal destinies.

MATTHEW 6:19-21

"Do not lay up for yourselves treasures on earth, where moth and rust destroy and where thieves break in and steal; but lay up for yourselves treasures in heaven, where neither moth nor rust destroys and where thieves do not break in and steal. For where your treasure is, there your heart will be also."

LUKE 12:29-31

"And do not seek what you should eat or what you should drink, nor have an anxious mind. For all these things the nations of the world seek after, and your Father knows that you need these things. But seek the kingdom of God, and all these things shall be added to you."

week
fourteen

As I give in today's offering, I have vision to see beyond my present circumstances, beyond my present problems or crises, beyond my needs and my desires. By faith I see my God working on my behalf to open doors that have been shut, to open up my mind to new ideas and my heart to new passions. I give today with great expectation for my God to do the impossible.

2 CORINTHIANS 5:7

For we walk by faith, not by sight.

1 CORINTHIANS 16:13

Watch, stand fast in the faith, be brave,
be strong.

HEBREWS 11:1

Now faith is the substance of things hoped for,
the evidence of things not seen.

week
fifteen

AS I GIVE IN TODAY'S OFFERING, I STAND IN UNITY WITH GOD, HIS WORD AND THE HOLY SPIRIT. I STAND TOGETHER IN PRAYER AND AGREEMENT WITH THOSE IN MY HOUSE, BELIEVING GOD WILL DO EXCEEDINGLY, ABUNDANTLY ABOVE ALL THAT I COULD ASK OR IMAGINE. I STAND WITH MY SHIELD AND MY SWORD TO WAR AGAINST DOUBT AND UNBELIEF. I STAND AGAINST ALL THE POWERS OF THE ENEMY. I STAND IN MY PLACE AND WILL NOT BE MOVED. I WILL NOT GIVE UP!

EPHESIANS 6:11 & 13

Put on the whole armor of God, that you may be able to stand against the wiles of the devil... Therefore take up the whole armor of God, that you may be able to withstand in the evil day, and having done all, to stand.

2 CHRONICLES 20:17

"You will not need to fight in this battle. Position yourselves, stand still and see the salvation of the Lord, who is with you, O Judah and Jerusalem! Do not fear or be dismayed; tomorrow go out against them, for the Lord is with you."

week
sixteen

As I give in today's offering, I have faith in the God who created the heavens and the earth, the God who has given us His infallible word, the God who promises and never breaks His word. I have faith in my God who shall supply all that is needed, when it is needed. He is never late and never early, but always on time every time. I choose to put my trust in the Lord again today, right now.

ROMANS 12:3

For I say, through the grace given to me, to everyone who is among you, not to think of himself more highly than he ought to think, but to think soberly, as God has dealt to each one a measure of faith.

HEBREWS 11:6

Without faith it is impossible to please Him, for he who comes to God must believe that He is, and that He is a rewarder of those who diligently seek Him.

week
seventeen

As I give in today's offering, I commit myself to the written Word of God. I seek to obey His Word and to put it into practice, not excusing myself by my own reasoning. I choose to honor His Word above my thoughts, desires or arguments. God deserves my respect and obedience. I give today with an obedient spirit and attitude.

ISAIAH 1:19

"If you are willing and obedient, you shall eat the good of the land."

PHILIPPIANS 2:8

And being found in appearance as a man, He humbled Himself and became obedient to the point of death, even the death of the cross.

week
eighteen

AS I GIVE IN TODAY'S OFFERING, I WILLINGLY GIVE TO THE LORD, NOT FROM GUILT OR COMPULSION, BUT FROM A WILLING HEART. I GIVE WITH A HEART THAT IS SINCERELY EXCITED ABOUT THE OPPORTUNITY TO GIVE FREELY AND ABUNDANTLY OF ALL I HAVE, A HEART THAT IS SOFT AND EASILY MOVED TOWARD THE WORK OF GOD. I LOVE YOU, LORD. I LOVE YOUR PEOPLE AND I LOVE THE CHURCH WHERE YOU HAVE PLACED ME.

EXODUS 25:2

"Speak to the children of Israel, that they bring Me an offering. From everyone who gives it willingly with his heart you shall take My offering."

EXODUS 35:21

Then everyone came whose heart was stirred, and everyone whose spirit was willing, and they brought the Lord's offering for the work of the tabernacle of meeting, for all its service, and for the holy garments.

EXODUS 35:5

"Take from among you an offering to the Lord. Whoever is of a willing heart, let him bring it as an offering to the Lord."

week
nineteen

As I give in today's offering, I give thanks to the God of my salvation, to the God who has shown me unmerited mercy and gives me a new heart, a new life, and a new destiny. Thank You, Lord, for all Your gracious provisions. I am amazed at how You are watching over every area of my life. I bring my offering this day with a thankful heart.

PSALM 79:13

So we, Your people and sheep of Your pasture, will give You thanks forever; We will show forth Your praise to all generations.

PSALM 106:1

Praise the Lord! Oh, give thanks to the Lord, for He is good! For His mercy endures forever.

week
twenty

As I give in today's offering, I commit myself to walk in the fear of the Lord with humility and sincerity and to respect, honor, and obey the Lord God Almighty. I repent of any independent attitude or pride and ask for God to keep me and bless me in every way. I give today with total confidence in my God.

PSALM 19:9

The fear of the Lord is clean, enduring forever; the judgments of the Lord are true and righteous altogether.

PSALM 33:8

Let all the earth fear the Lord; Let all the inhabitants of the world stand in awe of Him.

PSALM 115:11 & 13

You who fear the Lord, trust in the Lord; He is their help and their shield....He will bless those who fear the Lord, both small and great.

week
twenty one

As I give in today's offering, I resist all thoughts and feelings of anxiety, worry, or fear. I confess that I am a child of God. God knows me and loves me. God knows my smallest needs and my largest needs. God is faithful to watch over me like He watches over the birds of the air and the lilies of the field. I joyfully give today with faith and not with fear.

MATTHEW 6:25-30

"Therefore I say to you, do not worry about your life, what you will eat or what you will drink; nor about your body, what you will put on. Is not life more than food and the body more than clothing? Look at the birds of the air, for they neither sow nor reap nor gather into barns; yet your heavenly Father feeds them. Are you not of more value than they? Which of you by worrying can add one cubit to his stature? So why do you worry about clothing? Consider the lilies of the field, how they grow: they neither toil nor spin; and yet I say to you that even Solomon in all his glory was not arrayed like one of these. Now if God so clothes the grass of the field, which today is, and tomorrow is thrown into the oven, will He not much more clothe you, O you of little faith?"

week
twenty two

As I give in today's offering, I choose to give with a liberal spirit, a liberal heart, and open hand. I will not shrink back because or fear or greed. I will open my hand and give back to the Lord abundantly and generously. I will not allow a stingy spirit to overtake my heart.

ROMANS 12:8

He who exhorts, in exhortation; he who gives,
with liberality; he who leads, with diligence;
he who shows mercy, with cheerfulness.

2 CORINTHIANS 8:2

That in a great trial of affliction the abundance of
their joy and their deep poverty abounded in the
riches of their liberality.

week
twenty three

As I give in today's offering, I rejoice in the Lord and in the power of the Holy Spirit. I rejoice in good times and in bad times. I rejoice when I have abundance and when there is lack. I rejoice at all times and in every season, for God works in the darkness and the light, in the valley and on the mountain top. Although I may endure sufferings and trials, I have decided to stand my ground of faith. I give today joyfully, liberally, and sacrificially, knowing my God is faithful.

HABAKKUK 3:18

Yet I will rejoice in the Lord, I will joy in the God of my salvation.

PSALM 5:11

But let all those rejoice who put their trust in You.

PSALM 31:7

I will be glad and rejoice in Your mercy, for You have considered my trouble; You have known my soul in adversities...

week
twenty four

As I give in today's offering, I reflect on the greatness and power of my God. God is capable of doing anything. No task is too large or too difficult for Him. His power is never restrained. God is all-powerful. He does what He chooses to do, whenever and wherever. God is watching over me and He supplies for me by His power. Nothing is too difficult for God.

PSALM 147:5

Great is our Lord, and mighty in power;
His understanding is infinite.

PSALM 59:16

But I will sing of Your power; Yes, I will sing
aloud of Your mercy in the morning; for You
have been my defense and refuge in the day of
my trouble.

PSALM 86:10

For You are great, and do wondrous things;
You alone are God.

week
twenty five

As I give in today's offering, I have faith in the all-knowing God I serve. He knows everything and His knowledge is totally true and accurate. There is nothing too hard for Him. He is never surprised. God has a clear understanding of my life, my problems, my challenges, and my resources. God knows how to take care of me.

ISAIAH 46:9-10

"Remember the former things of old, for I am God, and there is no other; I am God, and there is none like Me, declaring the end from the beginning, and from ancient times things that are not yet done, saying, 'My counsel shall stand, and I will do all My pleasure.'"

PSALM 139:1-6

O Lord, You have searched me and known me. You know my sitting down and my rising up; You understand my thought afar off. You comprehend my path and my lying down, and are acquainted with all my ways. For there is not a word on my tongue, but behold, O Lord, You know it altogether. You have hedged me behind and before, and laid Your hand upon me. Such knowledge is too wonderful for me; it is high, I cannot attain it.

week
twenty six

As I give in today's offering, I recognize that God is sovereignly involved in directing my life. I understand that I may make my plans but it is the Lord who directs my feet. God carefully oversees all that happens to me. No event or experience escapes His attention. I give today with a confidence in the sovereignty of God. The job I have, the business I run, and the money that comes through my hands are under the direction of God Almighty. It is not luck. It is not chance. It is God working on my behalf.

PROVERBS 19:21

There are many plans in a man's heart,
nevertheless the Lord's counsel—that will stand.

ROMANS 8:28

And we know that all things work together for
good to those who love God, to those who are
called according to His purpose.

1 PETER 5:7

Casting all your care upon Him, for He cares
for you.

week
twenty seven

As I give in today's offering, I give because God has first given to me. God has given me His love and forgiveness. He has given me all things that pertain to life and godliness. God has been a liberal giver, holding back nothing. He gives into my life even when I don't deserve it. Now I have one small opportunity to give back, to give with thankfulness out of what God has already given to me. Lord, here is my tithe and offerings. Take this small seed and multiply it many times for your work.

GENESIS 13:17

"Arise, walk in the land through its length and its width, for I give it to you."

PSALM 37:4

Delight yourself also in the Lord, and He shall give you the desires of your heart.

2 CORINTHIANS 9:7

Let each one give as he purposes in his heart, not grudgingly or of necessity; for God loves a cheerful giver.

week
twenty eight

AS I GIVE IN TODAY'S OFFERING, I GIVE FREELY WITH A THANKFUL ATTITUDE. I GIVE FREELY WITH NO RESTRAINTS UPON MY HEART. FREELY I HAVE RECEIVED AND FREELY I GIVE. LORD, TODAY IS MY DAY TO BE A JOYFUL, LIBERAL GIVER FOR YOU HAVE FREELY GIVEN TO ME ALL THINGS. I AM WALKING IN FREEDOM TODAY.

EZRA 2:68

Some of the heads of the fathers' houses, when they came to the house of the Lord which is in Jerusalem, offered freely for the house of God, to erect it in its place.

MATTHEW 10:8

Heal the sick, cleanse the lepers, raise the dead, cast out demons. Freely you have received, freely give.

2 CORINTHIANS 8:3

For I bear witness that according to their ability, yes, and beyond their ability, they were freely willing.

week
twenty nine

As I give in today's offering, Lord, I bring you what seems to me to be very little, but I know You can take what is little and make it much. You can take what I have and increase it for Your work and for my needs. Thank you, Lord, for being the God who is not limited by what I give.

1 KINGS 17:12-14

So she said, "As the Lord your God lives, I do not have bread, only a handful of flour in a bin, and a little oil in a jar; and see, I am gathering a couple of sticks that I may go in and prepare it for myself and my son, that we may eat it, and die." And Elijah said to her, "Do not fear; go and do as you have said, but make me a small cake from it first, and bring it to me; and afterward make some for yourself and your son. For thus says the Lord God of Israel: 'The bin of flour shall not be used up, nor shall the jar of oil run dry, until the day the Lord sends rain on the earth.'"

week
thirty

As I give in today's offering, I remember Your promises to me because You are the God of miracles and the God of provision. I remember today that You are the reason I am blessed. You have given me the strength to work, start my business, finish my schooling, invest my resources. You are the reason for all of my blessings.

DEUTERONOMY 8:18

"And you shall remember the Lord your God, for it is He who gives you power to get wealth, that He may establish His covenant which He swore to your fathers, as it is this day."

PSALM 77:11

I will remember the works of the Lord; surely I will remember Your wonders of old.

week
thirty one

AS I GIVE IN TODAY'S OFFERING, I STAND ON MY
GROUND OF FAITH AND WILL NOT BE MOVED.
I HAVE GIVEN MY TITHE AND MY OFFERINGS IN
FAITH. NOW I STAND MY GROUND, EXPECTING
GOD TO WORK WITH MY FAITH. I RESIST THE
ATTACKERS THAT WOULD DIMINISH MY FAITH.
I SHALL NOT BE MOVED.

PSALM 16:8

I have set the Lord always before me; because He is at my right hand I shall not be moved.

PSALM 55:22

Cast your burden on the Lord, and He shall sustain you; He shall never permit the righteous to be moved.

week
thirty two

AS I GIVE IN TODAY'S OFFERING, I TAKE MY
TITHE AND MY SPECIAL OFFERINGS AND GIVE
THEM TO THE WORK OF THE LORD BECAUSE
I BELIEVE GOD'S WORK IS GREAT AND EXTENSIVE
AND DESERVES MY FULL-HEARTED SUPPORT.
I GIVE EXPECTING GOD TO DO MIGHTY THINGS IN
THE MIDST OF HIS PEOPLE. HERE, LORD, TAKE
MY PART AND MULTIPLY IT TO DO YOUR WORK.

EXODUS 35:21

*Then everyone came whose heart was stirred,
and everyone whose spirit was willing, and they
brought the Lord's offering for the work of the
tabernacle of meeting, for all its service, and for
the holy garments.*

NEHEMIAH 4:19

*Then I said to the nobles, the rulers, and the rest
of the people, "The work is great and extensive,
and we are separated far from one another on
the wall."*

week
thirty three

As I give in today's offering, Lord, by faith I seek to give liberally and abundantly to Your house and to Your vision. I believe You desire to bless me with abundance, with more than enough. Lord, by faith I receive into my heart an abundant giving faith spirit and begin today to be a person of abundance.

1 CHRONICLES 29:16

O Lord our God, all this abundance that we have prepared to build You a house for Your holy name is from Your hand, and is all Your own.

ISAIAH 60:5

"Then you shall see and become radiant, and your heart shall swell with joy; because the abundance of the sea shall be turned to you, the wealth of the Gentiles shall come to you."

week
thirty four

As I give in today's offering, I rejoice in the faithfulness of God in and around my life. You have always watched over me, protected me, guided me, and provided for me. You are faithful and I am grateful. I bring my tithes and offerings with faith in your faithfulness to use it mightily.

PSALM 89:5

And the heavens will praise Your wonders, O Lord; Your faithfulness also in the assembly of the saints.

LAMENTATIONS 3:22-23

Through the Lord's mercies we are not consumed, because His compassions fail not. They are new every morning; great is Your faithfulness.

week
thirty five

As I give in today's offering, I have a vision for the house you are building, a house made of redeemed people from every walk of life, from all ages and from different places, a people of prayer and praise and a people of love and forgiveness. Thank you, Lord, for giving me the opportunity to give my tithes and offerings to build a great house.

ISAIAH 2:2

Now it shall come to pass in the latter days that the mountain of the Lord's house shall be established on the top of the mountains, and shall be exalted above the hills; and all nations shall flow to it.

1 KINGS 8:13

I have surely built You an exalted house, and a place for You to dwell in forever.

week
thirty six

As I give in today's offering, I bring the first fruits from all I have received from the hand of the Lord—the first fruits from my wages, the first fruits from my investments, the first fruits of anything and everything I have. I give in thankfulness for the harvest I have already reaped and in faith for the harvest I am going to reap.

2 CHRONICLES 31:5

As soon as the commandment was circulated, the children of Israel brought in abundance the first fruits of grain and wine, oil and honey, and of all the produce of the field; and they brought in abundantly the tithe of everything.

MATTHEW 6:33

But seek first the kingdom of God and His righteousness, and all these things shall be added to you.

week
thirty seven

As I give in today's offering, I thank God that I am a new person in Christ. I have received a new heart and a new spirit. My old nature is stubborn, stingy and selfish, but my new heart is yielding, agreeable and generous. My new life is one of serving and obeying God. Thank You, Lord, that You made me a new person.

EZEKIEL 36:26

"I will give you a new heart and put a new spirit within you; I will take the heart of stone out of your flesh and give you a heart of flesh."

2 CORINTHIANS 5:17

Therefore, if anyone is in Christ, he is a new creation; old things have passed away; behold, all things have become new.

week
thirty eight

As I give in today's offering, I confess that my money is a trust from God and must be earned and managed according to biblical principles. Jesus, You are Lord over my life including my finances. By God's grace, I determine to be generous, liberal and consistent with my giving. Help me, Lord, to be a faithful servant.

PSALM 24:1-2

The earth is the Lord's and all its fullness, the world and those who dwell therein. For He has founded it upon the seas, and established it upon the waters.

PSALM 50:1-2

The Mighty one, God the Lord, has spoken and called the earth from the rising of the sun to its going down. Out of Zion, the perfection of beauty, God will shine forth.

week
thirty nine

As I give in today's offering, I honor You, Lord, with the first part of my income and with all you put into my hands. All I have and all I possess is already Yours. You are the giver of all good things and therefore I give to You my first and my best. I hold nothing back. I give my tithe willingly and joyfully.

PROVERBS 3:9-10

Honor the Lord with your possessions, and with the firstfruits of all your increase; So your barns will be filled with plenty, and your vats will overflow with new wine.

1 CHRONICLES 29:9

Then the people rejoiced, for they had offered willingly, because with a loyal heart they had offered willingly to the Lord.

week
forty

As I give in today's offering, I give with a heart of faith. I give that which I already have set aside for the Lord, my tithe and my offerings. I give believing that God will use my gifts for His purposes and that God will enlarge my faith to become a pipeline for God's provisions. Use me, Lord. Pour through me. Let your abundance flow through me.

1 CORINTHIANS 16:2

On the first day of the week let each one of
you lay something aside, storing up as he may
prosper.

ROMANS 4:20

He did not waver at the promise of God through
unbelief, but was strengthened in faith, giving
glory to God.

week
forty one

As I give in today's offering, I remember all the good things You have done for me. I remember Your great mercy that You freely gave me when I did not deserve it. I remember receiving Your blessings and Your abundance. You caused me to prosper in my way. You gave me the power to achieve. I will not forget all Your benefits and goodness toward my life. I give today with a heart filled with thanksgiving.

PSALM 50:14

"Offer to God thanksgiving, and pay your vows to the Most High."

PSALM 136:1

Oh, give thanks to the Lord, for He is good! For His mercy endures forever.

PSALM 103:2

Bless the Lord, O my soul, and forget not all His benefits.

week
forty two

As I give in today's offering, I rejoice in your goodness toward my life and toward those around me. You, O Lord, are a good God who does good things all the time. I am amazed at Your love and constant mercy. I am amazed at how You watch over every detail of my life. Again today, I surrender my life to You. My plans, my decisions, my finances—I put them all into Your hands.

PSALM 65:9-11

You visit the earth and water it, You greatly enrich it; the river of God is full of water; You provide their grain, for so You have prepared it. You water its ridges abundantly, You settle its furrows; You make it soft with showers, You bless its growth. You crown the year with Your goodness, and Your paths drip with abundance.

EXODUS 34:6-7

And the Lord passed before him and proclaimed, "The Lord, the Lord God, merciful and gracious, longsuffering, and abounding in goodness and truth, keeping mercy for thousands, forgiving iniquity and transgression and sin, by no means clearing the guilty, visiting the iniquity of the fathers upon the children and the children's children to the third and the fourth generation."

week
forty three

As I give in today's offering, I believe that Your kingdom is eternal and that I am an eternal being created in Your image. I am passing through this world. I am a visitor. This is not my destination. I live with a vision for eternal things and to extend Your kingdom. Help me to let go of what is temporary and to lay hold of what is eternal. I give today with faith and vision for my future.

2 CORINTHIANS 4:17-18

For our light affliction, which is but for a moment, is working for us a far more exceeding and eternal weight of glory, while we do not look at the things which are seen, but at the things which are not seen. For the things which are seen are temporary, but the things which are not seen are eternal.

1 TIMOTHY 6:18-19

Let them do good, that they be rich in good works, ready to give, willing to share, storing up for themselves a good foundation for the time to come, that they may lay hold on eternal life.

week
forty four

As I give in today's offering, I believe for breakthrough of all longstanding obstacles in my life, my family, and my finances. I give today in faith, expecting God to open new doors of opportunity for my life. I believe for the "Breaker" anointing to break-through into my God-ordained future.

PSALM 44:5

Through You we will push down our enemies;
through Your name we will trample those who
rise up against us.

ISAIAH 61:7

Instead of your shame you shall have double
honor, and instead of confusion they shall rejoice
in their portion. Therefore in their land they shall
possess double; everlasting joy shall be theirs.

week
forty five

As I give in today's offering, I fix my eyes on Jesus, my Lord, my Savior and my Redeemer, my very present help in time of trouble, my song in the valley, my light in the darkness. My eyes are fixed. By faith I will not be moved. I will not be distracted. My giving is one way I use to say, "Jesus, I trust You and know You are working on my behalf."

HEBREWS 12:1-2

Therefore we also, since we are surrounded by so great a cloud of witnesses, let us lay aside every weight, and the sin which so easily ensnares us, and let us run with endurance the race that is set before us, looking unto Jesus, the author and finisher of our faith, who for the joy that was set before Him endured the cross, despising the shame, and has sat down at the right hand of the throne of God.

PSALM 16:8-9

I have set the Lord always before me; because He is at my right hand I shall not be moved. Therefore my heart is glad, and my glory rejoices; my flesh also will rest in hope.

week
forty six

As I give in today's offering, I believe in the supernatural power of God to multiply what I give to meet the needs in my church and in my life. I give with a spirit of expectation and faith. This is my kingdom investment and I believe the bank of heaven and all its resources will be released.

JOHN 6:11-12

And Jesus took the loaves, and when He had given thanks He distributed them to the disciples, and the disciples to those sitting down; and likewise of the fish, as much as they wanted. So when they were filled, He said to His disciples, "Gather up the fragments that remain, so that nothing is lost."

PHILIPPIANS 4:19

And my God shall supply all your needs according to His riches in glory by Christ Jesus.

week
forty seven

As I give in today's offering, I am grateful for my local church and the vision we have to reach the lost, to preach the gospel and to see many people restored to Christ. I seize this opportunity to give of my resources and help support the God-honoring work we are doing together.

MATTHEW 16:18-19

"And I also say to you that you are Peter, and on this rock I will build My church, and the gates of Hades shall not prevail against it. And I will give you the keys of the kingdom of heaven, and whatever you bind on earth will be bound in heaven, and whatever you loose on earth will be loosed in heaven."

2 CORINTHIANS 8:3-4

They gave as much as they could afford and even more, simply because they wanted to. They even asked and begged us to let them have the joy of giving their money for God's people.
(Contemporary English Version)

week
forty eight

As I give in today's offering, I give willingly and joyfully. We are made rich in every way in order to be generous on every occasion. I have no regrets for being generous. I have no intention of going back to being selfish or stingy. I give today with absolute joy in being a generous giver.

2 CORINTHIANS 8:7

But as you abound in everything—in faith, in speech, in knowledge, in all diligence, and in your love for us—see that you abound in this grace also.

2 CORINTHIANS 9:5

Therefore I thought it necessary to exhort the brethren to go to you ahead of time, and prepare your generous gift beforehand, which you had previously promised, that it may be ready as a matter of generosity and not as a grudging obligation.

week
forty nine

As I give in today's offering, I seek to be enlarged in my spirit and in my mind. I want to see more, believe more, do more, and be more than I have in the past. Today is my day to say, "Lord, enlarge my faith and vision. Stretch my spirit of giving. Allow me to move into another level of giving beyond my own capacity."

ISAIAH 54:2-3

"Enlarge the place of your tent, and let them stretch out the curtains of your dwellings; do not spare; lengthen your cords, and strengthen your stakes. For you shall expand to the right and to the left, and your descendants will inherit the nations, and make the desolate cities inhabited."

ISAIAH 55:10-11

"For as the rain comes down, and the snow from heaven, and do not return there, but water the earth, and make it bring forth and bud, that it may give seed to the sower and bread to the eater, so shall My word be that goes forth from My mouth; It shall not return to Me void, but it shall accomplish what I please, and it shall prosper in the thing for which I sent it."

week
fifty

As I give in today's offering, let me not despise the day of small beginnings. Everything begins with a small seed, yet it grows and reproduces many times. Let my seed be planted today. Although it may look small, I believe it will grow and multiply.

JOB 8:7

Though your beginning was small, yet your latter end would increase abundantly.

1 KINGS 18:44

Then it came to pass the seventh time, that he said, "There is a cloud, as small as a man's hand, rising out of the sea!" So he said, "Go up, say to Ahab 'Prepare your chariot, and go down before the rain stops you.'"

week
fifty one

AS I GIVE IN TODAY'S OFFERING, I STAND HAND IN HAND WITH THE BELIEVERS THAT MAKE UP OUR COVENANT COMMUNITY. TOGETHER WE CAN MAKE A DIFFERENCE. TOGETHER WE CAN ACCOMPLISH GREAT THINGS FOR THE KINGDOM OF GOD. I AM ONE GIVER, YET I GIVE WITH THE WHOLE CONGREGATION AS ONE CHURCH, PRESENTING TO THE LORD ONE OFFERING, GIVEN IN UNITY OF HEART.

ACTS 4:32-33

Now the multitude of those who believed were of one heart and one soul; neither did anyone say that any of the things he possessed was his own, but they had all things in common. And with great power the apostles gave witness to the resurrection of the Lord Jesus. And great grace was upon them all.

EPHESIANS 4:16

From whom the whole body, joined and knit together by what every joint supplies, according to the effective working by which every part does its share, causes growth of the body for the edifying of itself in love.

week
fifty two

I CONSIDER IT A PRIVILEGE TO BE A CHANNEL FOR YOUR ABUNDANT SUPPLY. I WILL NOT STOP THE FLOW OF YOUR RESOURCES. ALL THAT YOU PUT INTO MY HANDS IS TO BE USED WISELY AND INVESTED CAREFULLY INTO YOUR KINGDOM. I KNOW THAT NO MATTER HOW MUCH I PASS ON, THERE WILL ALWAYS BE MORE COMING TO ME AND THROUGH ME.

2 CORINTHIANS 9:7-8

So let each one give as he purposes in his heart, not grudgingly or of necessity; for God loves a cheerful giver. And God is able to make all grace abound toward you, that you, always having all sufficiency in all things, may have an abundance for every good work.

PROVERBS 11:24-25

There is one who scatters, yet increases more; and there is one who withholds more than is right, but it leads to poverty. The generous soul will be made rich, and he who waters will also be watered himself.

Teaching Resources

A Call to Tithing

The Biblical Responsibility
of Every Believer

PROVERBS 3:9-10

Honor the Lord with your possessions, and with the firstfruits of all your increase; So your barns will be filled with plenty, and your vats will overflow with new wine.

INTRODUCTION

We need a biblical reorientation about finances and our possessions. Our giving is a spiritual matter that involves the heart, our spiritual knowledge of scriptures, and our spiritual capacity for faith in God and His invisible powers. Giving reflects our value system, our life priorities, and our life disciplines. Seeing God work in our material world of things will enlarge our faith for the invisible world of the kingdom of God. Our old nature is stubborn, stingy, selfish, doubting, and reasoning. It takes the act of salvation to create a new heart and a new nature that loves to give.

I. THE OLD AND THE NEW IN CONFLICT
(Proverbs 11:24)

A. The Old Nature: Withholds more than is right

B. The New Nature: Scatters and increases (Ezekiel 36:26; 2 Corinthians 5:17; Colossians 3:10)

II. CULTIVATING A GIVING LIFESTYLE

A. Stewardship: A steward is a guardian of the interests of another. He owns nothing, but is careful to guard, protect, and increase the property of the one he serves. We are stewards of time, strength and ability, as well as our money. (Luke 16:1-13)

B. Giving: Giving activates divine law that releases the work of God in our private world. "Honor the Lord with your substance and with the first fruits of all your increase." (Proverbs 3:9)

C. Receiving: God responds to our giving by opening up opportunities to receive divine provisions both directly and indirectly from His hand "So your barns will be filled with plenty." (Proverbs 3:10a)

D. Prospering: God desires that we receive abundantly and have more than enough so as to become liberal givers. "Your vats will overflow with new wine." (Proverbs 3:10b)

III. CULTIVATING A RIGHT PERSPECTIVE ABOUT OUR GIVING
(Deuteronomy 26:1-9)

A. Remember God's Goodness Before Giving (Deuteronomy 26:1-4)

B. Remember Our Life Before God Saved Us
(Deuteronomy 26:5-7)

C. Remember God's Mercy in Delivering Us
(Deuteronomy 26:8)
1. Divine Love: "The Lord brought us out"
2. Divine Power: "By His mighty hand"
3. Divine Intervention: "Signs and wonders"

D. Celebrate With Gratefulness Our New
Blessed Life
(Deuteronomy 26:9)
1. Spiritual Freedom: "Brought us out"
2. Spiritual Inheritance: "Given us the land"
3. Spiritual Provision: "Flowing with milk and honey"

IV. CULTIVATING FAITH AND OBEDIENCE FOR GIVING OUR TITHE
(Deuteronomy 26:10-15)

Tithe: Tithe is the tenth part of anything. It is the first part of our income, of all we earn, and it already belongs to the Lord. This is our first giving responsibility and our minimum financial commitment.

A. Tithe is the first of our wages and the first of our increase.
   (Deuteronomy 26:10; Proverbs 3:9-10)

B. Tithe is the acknowledgement that all we have belongs to the Lord.
   (Deuteronomy 26:10; 8:11-20; Genesis 28:22)

C. Tithe is to be given with an attitude of worship as a rejoicing offering.
   (Deuteronomy 26:10; 2 Corinthians 9:7; John 12:3-5; Leviticus 22:17-22, 29)

D. Tithe is to be given from our increase also.
   (Deuteronomy 26:12)

E. Tithe is the sacred portion that we set aside as the Lord's. It is holy.
(Deuteronomy 26:13; Leviticus 27:26-33)

F. Tithe is not to be used for personal needs.
(Deuteronomy 26:14; Leviticus 27:30)

G. Tithe is to be given as an act of spiritual obedience.
(Deuteronomy 26:14)

H. Tithe is one aspect that resists the curses that can affect our lives.
(Deuteronomy 26:15; 26:19;
Malachi 3:8-11; Luke 6:38)

I. Tithe is the provision for the releasing of ministry in the house of the Lord.
(Nehemiah 13:10-12; 1 Corinthians 9:9;
Acts 28:10)

J. Tithing is not just Old Testament teaching; both Jesus and the Apostles confirmed tithing and giving offerings.
(Matthew 23:23; 6:1; 1 Corinthians 16:1-2)

K. Tithing is a biblical minimum and will not limit our giving but opens the door to genuine stewardship.

L. Tithing is the acknowledgement of ownership that God is owner of all and that we are only stewards and trustees over our human estates.

M. Tithing is a token of consecration that one has surrendered all and made Him Lord.

V. CULTIVATING A PRAYER-WARFARE STANCE WITH YOUR TITHING ACT

A. Repent of withholding and remove the blessing blockage.
(Malachi 3:8-9)

B. Bring the tithe into the storehouse.
(Genesis 41:56; Deuteronomy 28:8)

C. Stand with the promises of God for the tithe.
(Proverbs 10:6; 28:20; Malachi 3:10; Genesis 12:2)
1. Blessings multiply.
2. Open the shut windows of heaven.
3. Pour out a personalized, custom-made blessing.
4. Enlarge your blessing beyond your capacity to receive.

5. Blessings upon your work.

6. The Lord will rebuke the devourer.

7. Stand with the authority of God for continued blessings.

Believing in the Principle of Receiving

God responds to our faith and our giving by opening up new opportunities to receive divine provisions both directly and indirectly from His hand.

INTRODUCTION

The principle of receiving is scriptural, as is the
principle of reaping. Reaping is receiving, reaping
is fulfillment, reaping is finishing the course, reaping is the receiver's reward. Seeds always produce
more than what is planted, so it is in God's economy. We plant the seed. Life and work waters it,
but God ultimately gives the increase. We are posi-
tioning ourselves for increase, both individually
and corporately. We are believing to receive our
full portion. We come with open hearts and open
hands, prayerfully saying, "God, pour into our
hands your sovereign, divine provision." Scripture
says, "Everyone who asks, receives." We are asking

for increase, blessing, multiplication, and miracles. God, you desire to bless us and we desire to receive. We sow not only money, but also prayer, faith, and evangelism. The world is in desperate need and there are souls we need to harvest for Christ. The advance of the gospel requires the investment of dedicated believers. We choose to advance, knowing it requires more resources to reach our region and beyond. It takes you, the believer, to become a giver and a receiver. To give without faith to receive cuts the process in half. (Malachi 3:10; Mark 10:30; Matthew 7:8)

I. THE ATTITUDE OF A RECEIVER

    A. Defining the Word "Receive"
       (Acts 3:5; Matthew 7:8; Psalm 24:5; John 16:24)
       1. *Lambano*: to take or receive with open hands, accepting.
       2. *Paralambano*: to receive from another, to take.

3. *Analambano*: to take to oneself, to hold on to.

4. *Apolambano*: to receive as one's due, expecting results on what has been invested or sown.

5. *Proslambano*: to receive with special interest on the part of the receiver, to welcome with open arms.

6. *Metalambano*: to have or get a share of, to partake.

7. *Hupolambano*: to take and bear up under what is taken in or on, to prepare to carry the load.

8. *Dechomai*: to receive by deliberate and ready reception of what is offered, to take hold with the hand, firmly grasping.

9. *Anadechomai*: to receive gladly, taking responsibility as the receiver; faith in the promise.

10. *Apodechomai*: to welcome, to receive gladly, to receive without reserve.

11. *Apecho*: to have in full, to have received, to see the end result as having already received.

12. *Choreo*: to make room for what is to be received.

B. Summary and Working Definition

The attitude of receiving is to take and receive with open hands, by faith making room for and receiving by deliberate and ready reception of all that God is bringing into your hands.

II. WAYS IN WHICH A BELIEVER RECEIVES

A. Receive from your work or business.

B. Receive from your wise decisions and investments.

C. Receive from surprise blessings and hidden protections.

D. God will withhold no good thing from us. (Psalm 84:11)

This promise is one that should go before your eyes on a daily basis. The Lord our God is a good God, a God who does not withhold, a God who enjoys releasing good things into our lives.

1. Five prerequisites to receiving the promise:
   a. Be a person who loves the presence of God
   b. Be a person who loves God's house
   c. Be a person who pushes through
   d. Be a person of prayer and devotion
   e. Be a person of integrity

2. What good things can you receive from our good God?
   a. Good treasure
      (Deuteronomy 28:12)
   b. Good life (Deuteronomy 30:15)
   c. Good hand of God on me
      (Nehemiah 2:8)
   d. Good taste (Psalm 34:8)
   e. Good things (Psalm 34:10)
   f. Good reward (Ecclesiastes 4:9)
   g. Good gifts (Matthew 7:11)
   h. Good works in you
      (Philippians 1:6)

III. THE RECEIVER BELIEVES THE PROMISES

A. The promise is a pledge, a word of honor, a vow, oath, warranty, guarantee, covenant. It is the ground for hope, expectation, assurance of eventual success.
   (Romans 4:20)

B. The Promiser is God and His Word

The promiser is God who is all powerful, all knowing, creator, provider. He is a God who works miracles and who is generous in His blessings.

(Numbers 23:19; 1 Kings 8:56; Hebrews 6:18)

IV. THE RECEIVER'S COMMITMENT

A. A commitment to enlarging my prayers and my asking.

B. A commitment to living by faith and not by sight.

C. A commitment to standing in times of testing.

D. A commitment to rejoicing as I see the provision on its way.

Faith to be a Great Giver

*A Great Giver's Heart
with a Great Giver's Faith
Will Result in Great Giving*

INTRODUCTION

The Bible portrays God as a great giver, liberal with His resources, always ready to give abundantly into the needs of His people. We are created in the image of God. We are also capable of being great givers. I believe giving is opposite to our human nature, especially our unredeemed carnal nature. To be a great giver you need a new nature, a Holy Spirit-empowered nature with an attitude of faith and expectation. We at City Bible Church seek to become a people who have a giving spirit. A great giver's heart with a great giver's faith will result in great giving. Our motive for great giving is to advance the kingdom of God. Giving to God is confronting our carnal nature, confronting our culture of greed, selfishness, credit madness, and unnecessary accumulation of things. As great givers, one expression is participating in the Faith Harvest giving, a time when all of us can focus on giving according to our faith, according to our vision for sowing liberally our seed.

(2 Corinthians 9:7-8; Psalm 115:14-15; Acts 20:35; Luke 17:5; Zechariah 8:12; Isaiah 30:23)

I. GREAT GIVER'S OPPORTUNITIES TO GIVE

A. Giving of Our Tithe: Tithe is a tenth of anything. It is the first part of our income, of all we earn, and it already belongs to the Lord. This is our first giving responsibility and our minimum financial commitment.

B. Giving of Our Offering: An offering is an undesignated, unlimited amount given as a free-will love gift unto the Lord. We are encouraged in Scripture to grow in the grace of giving. The tithe always remains the tithe, 10%, but offerings are unlimited giving. This is where we grow in liberality, generosity, faith, and sacrifice.

C. Giving of Our Faith Harvest Offering: A faith harvest offering is given by the believer with the knowledge that this seed is sowed in faith, believing God to water it and enable it to become the full harvest of what God desires to bring into his life. This is a faith offering, a specific giving with liberality and sacrifice.

II. PROVEN PRINCIPLES FOR GREAT GIVERS

A. Giving empowered by grace releases the favor of God upon the giver.
   (2 Corinthians 8:1)
   1. Grace
      a. Divine Enablement: God will enable you by giving strength to you.
      b. Divine Generosity: God will put generosity into your heart.

2. Grace Defined
   a. *Charis*: found ten times in II Corinthians 8-9, referring either to the divine generosity favorably displayed or to divine enablement to participate worthily in the collection.
   b. Favor: To dignify or raise by an act of favor, to honor, to bless, lift up, to supply with all that is needed.
3. Grace: our motivator/stimulator for giving
   a. It's grace that motivates us to give; grace initiates giving.
   b. It's grace, not law, not rules, not guilt, nor competition that stimulates a Christian to give.
   c. It's grace that gives us the ability to give, the desire to give, and motivation to move into faith.

B. Giving, in spite of the affliction of poverty, produces great joy and releases supernatural provision.
    (2 Corinthians 8:2)
    1. Four kinds of poverty:
        a. Chastening poverty: violation of God's principles (Samson)
        b. Testing poverty: learning God's character (Job)
        c. Redemptive poverty: giving wealth to others
        d. Attitude poverty: realizing our need for God or seeing needs but lacking the attitude of faith for change.
    2. Example of one who gave out of poverty (Mark 12:42-43)

C. Giving beyond one's ability, without thought of oneself, breaks the spirit of poverty.
    (2 Corinthians 8:3)

D. Giving in spite of human restraints or human reasoning overcomes smallness of spirit.
(2 Corinthians 8:4)

E. Giving sacrificially deepens dependence upon God as our only source.
(2 Corinthians 8:5; Philippians 4:19; 1 Kings 17:12-14)

F. Giving should be proportionate to one's spiritual growth in other Christian virtues.
(2 Corinthians 8:7)

G. Giving that completes commitments which started with inspired faith will establish deep conviction for lifetime giving.
(2 Corinthians 8:8-11)

H. Giving is acceptable to God on the basis of the giver's heart, not the giver's amount.
(2 Corinthians 8:12)

I. Giving allows the Holy Spirit to minister to our deficiency.
   (2 Corinthians 8:13-15)

J. Giving can be snared by delayed obedience brought about by postponement of generosity.
   (2 Corinthians 9:1-5)

K. Giving with a joyful attitude pleases the heart of God.
   (2 Corinthians 9:7-8; Proverbs 22:9)

Financial Freedom

Financial freedom comes through managing my resources by biblical principles which allow God to bless me and to bless other people through me.

INTRODUCTION

God evaluates us as servants using His resources, not as owners using our own money and resources. Since all we do should glorify His name and extend His work on earth, how we go about using His money is crucial. It is the quality of financial management, not the quantity of finances managed. Godly biblical money management is a matter of how and not how much. It's not how much money you make but what you do with the money you have.

I. GOD USES MONEY TO TEACH US

A. To establish a dependence on the Lord and to trust Him.

B. To develop a spirit of gratefulness and contentment.

C. To teach us to live within our means.

D. To help us enjoy our life, possessions and blessings.

E. To give us direction by having or not having sufficient resources.

F. To determine who is the Lord of our life.

G. To manifest His supernatural power to us.

H. To deliver us from wrong motives and attitudes, He will take money from us.

II. WHAT IS FINANCIAL FREEDOM

A. Financial freedom is an attitude. Our attitude must be to use our resources to serve God, His church and others, not just to comfort ourselves.

1. Wrong Concept: Financial freedom is freedom for ourselves through freedom from others. It is the ability to retire early, be debt-free, and be financially independent. These are American lies.

2. Wrong Focus: His entire world is full of himself and his things. He cannot see the need for others.

(Luke 12:17-19; Ecclesiastes 5:10-11)

B. Financial freedom is a decision and a discipline.

1. Must make a commitment to follow proven biblical principles.

2. Must make and follow a plan, strategizing to live according to biblical priorities.
3. Financial freedom is possible.

C. Scriptural Facts About My Finances
   1. Scripture clearly states you cannot take your possessions with you.
      (Ecclesiastes 5:15-16)
   2. Scripture clearly states you can know who you serve by how you use your money.
      (Luke 16:13)
   3. Scripture clearly states that greed is a life destroyer.
      (Luke 11:39; Proverbs 1:19; Proverbs 15:2)
   4. Scripture clearly states that God expects you to handle your money wisely.
      (Matthew 25:21-27; Proverbs 9:9)
   5. Scripture clearly states that you are responsible for all your decisions.
      (Galatians 6:7-8)

6. Scripture clearly states we should plan with difficulties in mind.
   (Ecclesiastes 7:14; Proverbs 22:3)

31 Financial Promises

The attitude of receiving is to take and receive with **open hands,** by faith making room for and receiving, by deliberate and ready reception, all that God is bringing into your hands.

AS YOU GIVE, YOU WILL INCREASE MORE.

Proverbs 11:24: "There is one who scatters, yet increases more; and there is one who withholds more than is right, but it leads to poverty."

AS YOU WATER, YOU WILL BE WATERED MORE.

Proverbs 11:25: "The generous soul will be made rich, and he who waters will also be watered himself."

AS YOU GIVE TO THE POOR, THE LORD PAYS YOU BACK.

Proverbs 19:17: "He who has pity on the poor lends to the Lord, and He will pay back what he has given."

AS YOU ARE FAITHFUL WITH LITTLE, GOD WILL PUT YOU IN CHARGE OF MUCH.

Matthew 25:21: "His lord said to him, 'Well done, good and faithful servant; you were faithful over a few things, I will make you ruler over many things. Enter into the joy of your lord.'"

AS YOU GIVE LIBERALLY, IT WILL BE GIVEN BACK TO YOU RUNNING OVER.

Luke 6:38: "Give, and it will be given to you: good measure, pressed down, shaken together, and running over will be put into your bosom. For with the same measure that you use, it will be measured back to you."

THERE WILL BE NO SORROW WITH YOUR WEALTH.

Proverbs 10:22: "The blessing of the Lord makes one rich, and He adds no sorrow with it."

YOUR LIFE WILL BE FILLED WITH PRECIOUS AND PLEASANT RICHES.

Proverbs 24:3-4: "Through wisdom a house is built, and by understanding it is established; by knowledge the rooms are filled with all precious and pleasant riches."

THE LORD WILL ABUNDANTLY BLESS YOUR PROVISIONS.

Palms 132:15: "I will abundantly bless her provision; I will satisfy her poor with bread."

YOUR BARNS WILL BE FILLED AND YOUR VATS WILL OVERFLOW.

Proverbs 3:9-10: "Honor the Lord with your possessions, and with the firstfruits of all your increase; So your barns will be filled with plenty, and your vats will overflow with new wine."

AS YOU SOW BOUNTIFULLY, YOU WILL REAP BOUNTIFULLY.

2 Corinthians 9:6-7: "But this I say: He who sows sparingly will also reap sparingly, and he who sows bountifully will also reap bountifully. So let each one give as he purposes in his heart, not grudgingly or of necessity; for God loves a cheerful giver."

AS YOU HAVE GENEROUS EYES, YOU WILL BE BLESSED ABUNDANTLY.

Proverbs 22:9: "He who has a generous eye will be blessed, for he gives of his bread to the poor."

YOU WILL HAVE NO LACK IN YOUR LIFE.

Proverbs 28:27: "He who gives to the poor will not lack, but he who hides his eyes will have many curses."

YOU WILL HAVE HOUSES AND RICHES THAT YOU WILL ENJOY.

Proverbs 19:14: "Houses and riches are an inheritance from fathers, but a prudent wife is from the Lord."

THE WEALTH OF SINNERS IS WAITING FOR YOU.

Proverbs 13:22: "A good man leaves an inheritance to his children's children, but the wealth of the sinner is stored up for the righteous."

THE MANY BLESSINGS OF GOD WILL OVERTAKE YOU.

Deuteronomy 28:2: "All these blessings shall come upon you and overtake you, because you obey the voice of the Lord your God."

YOU WILL HAVE OPEN WINDOWS OF HEAVEN.

Malachi 3:10: "'Bring all the tithes into the storehouse, that there may be food in My house, and try Me now in this,' says the Lord of hosts, 'If I will not open for you the windows of heaven and pour out for you such blessing that there will not be room enough to receive it.'"

THE LORD WILL GIVE YOU A SURPLUS OF PROSPERITY.

Deuteronomy 28:11: "The Lord will grant you plenty of goods, in the fruit of your body, in the increase of your livestock and in the produce of your ground, in the land of which the Lord swore to your fathers to give you."

GOD WILL MAKE YOUR WAY PROSPEROUS.

Joshua 1:8: "This Book of the Law shall not depart from your mouth, but you shall meditate in it day and night, that you may observe to do according to all that is written in it. For then you will make your way prosperous, and then you will have good success."

YOU WILL SPEND YOUR YEARS IN PROSPERITY AND PLEASURES.

Job 36:11: "If they obey and serve Him, they shall spend their days in prosperity, and their years in pleasures."

GOD WILL GIVE YOU THE DREAMS OF YOUR HEART.

Psalm 37:4: "Delight yourself also in the Lord, and He shall give you the desires of your heart."

WEALTH AND RICHES WILL BE IN YOUR HOUSE.

Psalm 112:3: "Wealth and riches will be in his house, and his righteousness endures forever."

GOD WILL GIVE YOU TREASURES HIDDEN IN DARKNESS.

Isaiah 45:3: "I will give you the treasures of darkness and hidden riches of secret places, that you may know that I, the Lord, who call you by your name, am the God of Israel."

YOU WILL FIND HIDDEN WEALTH IN SECRET PLACES.

Isaiah 45:3: "I will give you the treasures of darkness and hidden riches of secret places, that you may know that I, the Lord, who call you by your name, am the God of Israel."

YOU WILL ENJOY YOUR SEASONS OF ABUNDANCE.

Philippians 4:12: "I know how to be abased, and I know how to abound. Everywhere and in all things I have learned both to be full and to be hungry, both to abound and to suffer need."

GOD WILL LIBERALLY SUPPLY ALL YOUR NEEDS.

Philippians 4:19: "And my God shall supply all your need according to His riches in glory by Christ Jesus."

GOD WILL BLESS YOU EVEN IN A BAD ECONOMY.

Genesis 26:3,12: "Dwell in this land, and I will be with you and bless you; for to you and your descendants I give all these lands, and I will perform the oath which I swore to Abraham your father... Then Isaac sowed in that land, and reaped in the same year a hundredfold; and the Lord blessed him."

GOD WILL PROVIDE ALL THE SEED YOU NEED TO SOW.

2 Corinthians 9:10: "Now may He who supplies seed to the sower, and bread for food, supply and multiply the seed you have sown and increase the fruits of your righteousness."

GOD WILL CROWN YOUR YEAR WITH BOUNTY AND GOODNESS.

Psalm 65:11: "You crown the year with Your goodness, and Your paths drip with abundance."

THE LORD WILL MAKE YOU ABUNDANTLY PROSPEROUS IN YOUR WORK.

Deuteronomy 30:9: "The Lord your God will make you abound in all the work of your hand, in the fruit of your body, in the increase of your livestock, and in the produce of your land for good. For the Lord will again rejoice over you for good as He rejoiced over your fathers."

THE PROVISIONS OF GOD WILL NEVER RUN OUT.

1 Kings 17:14,16: "For thus says the Lord God of Israel: 'The bin of flour shall not be used up, nor shall the jar of oil run dry, until the day the Lord sends rain on the earth.' ... The bin of flour was not used up, nor did the jar of oil run dry, according to the word of the Lord which He spoke by Elijah."

GOD GIVES YOU POWER TO GET WEALTH.
Deuteronomy 8:18: "And you shall remember the Lord your God, for it is He who gives you power to get wealth, that He may establish His covenant which He swore to your fathers, as it is this day."

God responds to our faith and our giving
by opening up new opportunities
to receive divine provisions both directly
and indirectly from His hand.

Faith to Match the Times

*Prayer and Encouragement
for the Business Person*

Preserve the core values and stimulate progressive vision. Cherish the basics but don't compare basic business with basic faith. It is the consistency of faith that gives us direction, not just business planning. Everything can change about business— methods, technology, staff, strategy of business— but what does not change is the basic purpose of glorifying God, serving a kingdom purpose, and that special ingredient, faith.

Our Prayer

• God grant us faith to explore, create, discover, achieve, to change and to improve.

- God grant us a supernatural infusion of faith that matches the times and drives us forward.

- God grant the team supernatural wisdom to use the gift of faith above and beyond the ideas of men or the climate of the industry.

- God grant us the faith to put our stake into the ground and stay the course.

- God grant us a new spirit of faith to see the unlimited number of possibilities that surround us. God grant us a bold faith to set bold goals that will accomplish great things for God's kingdom.

- God grant us great faith to see the invisible, believe the incredible and receive the impossible.

- God grant us great faith to believe God to be a good God, a God of abundance, an "all things are possible" God.

- God grant us great faith to believe God is all-powerful, at all times, in every circumstance. He is a God who is able to do anything.

- God grant us the capacity to reach for the unreasonable and not stoop to only guarding what we have.

SCRIPTURE REFERENCES
Habakkuk 2:4, Matthew 9:29, Matthew 15:28, Matthew 17:20, Matthew 21:21, Acts 6:8, Romans 1:17, I Corinthians 2:5

And after him was Shammah the son of Agee the Hararite. The Philistines had gathered together into a troop where there was a piece of ground full of lentils. Then the people fled from the Philistines. But he stationed himself in the middle of the field, defended it, and killed the Philistines. And the Lord brought about a great victory. (II Samuel 23:11-12)

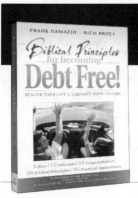
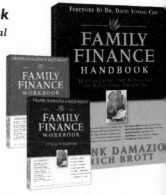